SandCastle 3

Homonyms

A Bat Hangs from the Bat

Kelly Doudna

Publishing Company

Published by SandCastle™, an imprint of ABDO Publishing Company, 4940 Viking Drive, Edina, Minnesota 55435.

Printed in the United States.

Photo credits: Corbis Images, Corel, Digital Vision, Eyewire Images, Image 100, PhotoDisc, Rubberball Productions

Library of Congress Cataloging-in-Publication Data

Doudna, Kelly, 1963-
    A bat hangs from the bat / Kelly Doudna.
      p. cm. -- (Homonyms)
    Includes index.
    Summary: Photographs and simple text introduce homonyms, words that are spelled and sound the same but have different meanings.
    ISBN 1-57765-785-3
      1. English language--Homonyms--Juvenile literature. [1. English language--Homonyms.] I. Title.

PE1595 .D68 2002
428.1--dc21

2001053325

The SandCastle concept, content, and reading method have been reviewed and approved by a national advisory board including literacy specialists, librarians, elementary school teachers, early childhood education professionals, and parents.

Let Us Know

After reading the book, SandCastle would like you to tell us your stories about reading. What is your favorite page? Was there something hard that you needed help with? Share the ups and downs of learning to read. We want to hear from you! To get posted on the Abdo Publishing Company Web site, send us email at:

sandcastle@abdopub.com

About SandCastle™
Nonfiction books for the beginning reader

- Basic concepts of phonics are incorporated with integrated language methods of reading instruction. Most words are short, and phrases, letter sounds, and word sounds are repeated.

- Book levels are based on the ATOS™ for Books formula. Other considerations for readability include the number of words in each sentence, the number of characters in each word, and word lists based on curriculum frameworks.

- Full-color photography reinforces word meanings and concepts.

- "Words I Can Read" list at the end of each book teaches basic elements of grammar, helps the reader recognize the words in the text, and builds vocabulary.

- Reading levels are indicated by the number of flags on the castle.

SandCastle uses the following definitions for this series:

- Homographs: words that are spelled the same but sound different and have different meanings. *Easy memory tip: "-graph"= same look*

- Homonyms: words that are spelled and sound the same but have different meanings. *Easy memory tip: "-nym"= same name*

- Homophones: words that sound alike but are spelled differently and have different meanings. *Easy memory tip: "-phone"= sound alike*

Look for more SandCastle books in these three reading levels:

Level 1 (one flag)	**Level 2** (two flags)	**Level 3** (three flags)

Grades Pre-K to K 5 or fewer words per page	**Grades K to 1** 5 to 10 words per page	**Grades 1 to 2** 10 to 15 words per page

bark   bark

Homonyms are words that are spelled and sound the same but have different meanings.

I am on the soccer team.

We practice with a pink and black ball.

Dad and I are at the water park.

We have a **ball** playing together.

I earned some money helping with chores.

I save it in my piggy bank.

My family and I camp.

We pitch our tent on the **bank** of the river.

I like to play baseball.

I am a good batter.

I am helping Mom make a cake.

I stir the batter.

The white stripe on the face of a horse
is a blaze.

Lightning struck this forest and started a fire.

It will blaze for a long time.

I learn while I play.

I can spell words with my blocks.

The other team tries to score.

The goalie blocks the shot.

I dressed up my cat.

He wears a green bow.

I am learning to play the cello.

I stroke it with a bow.

I eat cereal for breakfast.

I put it in a bowl with milk.

Dad and I have fun together.

He teaches me how to bowl.

I ate some salad.

I cannot **bear** the thought of eating any more.

What kind of animal catches a fish from the river?

(bear)

Words I Can Read

Nouns

A noun is a person, place, or thing

animal (AN-uh-muhl) p. 21

ball (BAWL) pp. 6, 7

bank (BANGK) p. 9

bark (BARK) p. 4

baseball (BAYSS-bawl) p. 10

batter (BAT-ur) pp. 10, 11

bear (BAIR) p. 21

blaze (BLAYZ) p. 12

blocks (BLOKSS) p. 14

bow (BOH) pp. 16, 17

bowl (BOHL) p. 18

breakfast (BREK-fuhst) p. 18

cake (KAYK) p. 11

cat (KAT) p. 16

cello (CHEL-oh) p. 17

cereal (SIHR-ee-uhl) p. 18

chores (CHORZ) p. 8

face (FAYSS) p. 12

family (FAM-uh-lee) p. 9

fire (FIRE) p. 13

fish (FISH) p. 21

forest (FOR-ist) p. 13

fun (FUHN) p. 19

goalie (GOH-lee) p. 15

homonyms (HOM-uh-nimz) p. 5

horse (HORSS) p. 12

kind (KINDE) p. 21

lightning (LITE-ning) p. 13

meanings (MEE-ningz) p. 5

milk (MILK) p. 18

money (MUHN-ee) p. 8

piggy bank (PIG-ee BANGK) p. 8

river (RIV-ur) pp. 9, 21

salad (SAL-uhd) p. 20

shot (SHOT) p. 15

soccer team (SOK-ur TEEM) p. 6

stripe (STRIPE) p. 12

team (TEEM) p. 15

tent (TENT) p. 9

thought (THAWT) p. 20

time (TIME) p. 13

water park (WAW-tur PARK) p. 7

words (WURDZ) pp. 5, 14

Proper Nouns

A proper noun is the name of a person, place, or thing

Dad (DAD) pp. 7, 19

Mom (MOM) p. 11

Pronouns

A pronoun is a word that replaces a noun

he (HEE) pp. 16, 19

I (EYE) pp. 6, 7, 8, 9, 10, 11, 14, 16, 17, 18, 19, 20

it (IT) pp. 8, 13, 17, 18

me (MEE) p. 19

more (MOR) p. 20

that (THAT) p. 5

we (WEE) pp. 6, 7, 9

what (WUHT) p. 21

Verbs

A verb is an action or being word

am (AM) pp. 6, 10, 11, 17

are (AR) pp. 5, 7

ate (AYT) p. 20

bark (BARK) p. 4

bear (BAIR) p. 20

blaze (BLAYZ) p. 13

blocks (BLOKSS) p. 15

bowl (BOHL) p. 19

camp (KAMP) p. 9

can (KAN) p. 14

cannot (KAN-not) p. 20

catches (KACH-ez) p. 21

dressed up (DRESST UHP) p. 16

earned (URND) p. 8

eat (EET) p. 18

eating (EET-ing) p. 20

have (HAV) pp. 5, 7, 19

helping (HELP-ing) pp. 8, 11

is (IZ) p. 12

learn (LURN) p. 14

learning (LURN-ing) p. 17

like (LIKE) p. 10

make (MAYK) p. 11

pitch (PICH) p. 9

play (PLAY) pp. 10, 14, 17

playing (PLAY-ing) p. 7

practice (PRAK-tiss) p. 6

put (PUT) p. 18

save (SAYV) p. 8

score (SKOR) p. 15

sound (SOUND) p. 5

spell (SPEL) p. 14

spelled (SPELD) p. 5

started (START-ed) p. 13

stir (STUR) p. 11

stroke (STROHK) p. 17

struck (STRUHK) p. 13

teaches (TEECH-ez) p. 19

tries (TRIZE) p. 15

wears (WAIRZ) p. 16

will (WIL) p. 13

Adjectives

An adjective describes something

any (EN-ee) p. 20
black (BLAK) p. 6
different (DIF-ur-uhnt)
  p. 5
good (GUD) p. 10
green (GREEN) p. 16

long (LAWNG) p. 13
my (MYE) pp. 8, 9, 14, 16
other (UHTH-ur) p. 15
our (OUR) p. 9
pink (PINGK) p. 6

same (SAYM) p. 5
some (SUHM) pp. 8, 20
this (THISS) p. 13
white (WITE) p. 12

Adverbs

An adverb tells how, when, or where
something happens

together (tuh-GETH-ur)
  pp. 7, 19